are chickens stripy?

Amanda Leslie

LITTLE TIGER PRESS
London

D1356310

do
snakes
run?

are
elephants
small?

do
seals
hop?

are
fish
hairy?

hop?

hairy?

do
hippos
jump?

are
chickens
stripy?

do
birds
crawl?

are
cows
spotty?

do
monkeys
swim?

are
ducks
woolly?

do
penguins
dig?

who runs,
hops, jumps, crawls
swims and digs
and is small, hairy,
stripy, spotty
and woolly?